QuiLt ThiS!

PRACTICAL PATTERNS FOR EVERYDAY QUILTING

Lynda Smith

The American Quilter's Society (AQS), located in Paducah, Kentucky, is dedicated to promoting the accomplishments of today's quilters. Through its publications and events, AQS strives to honor today's quiltmakers and their work and to inspire future creativity and innovation in quiltmaking.

Text © 2008, Author, Lynda Smith
Artwork © 2008 American Quilter's Society

Editor: Andi Reynolds
Graphic Design: Lynda Smith
Cover Design: Michael Buckingham
Photography: Charles R. Lynch

American Quilter's Society
P. O. Box 3290 • Paducah, KY 42002-3290
www.americanquilter.com

Library of Congress Cataloging-in-Publication Data

Smith, Lynda, 1959-
   Quilt this! practical patterns for everyday quilting / by Lynda Smith.
      p. cm.
   ISBN 978-1-57432-967-4
   1. Quilting--Patterns. 2. Patchwork--Patterns. I. Title.

TT835.S5644 2008
746.46'041--dc22

2008031172

Proudly printed and bound in the United States of America.

Chapter page photos are courtesy of PDPhoto.org, publicdomainphotos.com, publicdomainpictures.net, and U.S. Fish and Wildlife Service.

Lynda Smith

Quilt This!

Dedication

To my husband, Donnie, for his never-ending love and support

and

my kids, Brian and Michael.

Acknowledgments

A special thanks to some very special friends:

Marge Boyle for suggesting I write this book

Bonnie Browning for being a great teacher and a dear friend

Andi Reynolds for being the best editor a girl could ever have

Meredith Schroeder for this great opportunity

Helen Squire for sharing her inspiration of quilting

Sally Terry for stitching the samples for this book

contents

Quilt This!

Lynda Smith

Foreword

I met Lynda Smith in 2000 when she joined the staff at the American Quilter's Society as a graphic designer. From those early days on the job, Lynda showed her prowess at drawing graphics and quilting designs on the computer. She has been the book designer on three of the nine books that AQS has published for me, including my latest book, *Borders & Finishing Touches* 2.

Lynda is no stranger to making quilts; she made baby quilts for her two sons who are now in their twenties. When she wanted to make a bed-sized quilt for her guest room, I volunteered to help her—translated that meant I would guide her through the process of making a quilt with appliqué and six borders. Lynda's husband, Donnie, teased her every time she came home with more sections stitched, saying, "Bonnie did good work!" But Lynda and I know that she stitched every piece together to make LOVELY PINK, including all of those mitered corners on the borders.

But our collaboration didn't end there. Lynda and I appliquéd MERDIE'S POPPIES, a quilt to celebrate Bill and Meredith Schroeder's fiftieth wedding anniversary. This quilt was presented to them at the AQS Quilt Expo in Nashville, after we presented a gag quilt to them.

Today this special quilt hangs in Meredith's office.

What does this story have to do with this book? Besides learning how important marking and pinning are in making a quilt, Lynda also saw firsthand the importance of scale and how the quilting designs need to fill the space. Next thing I knew, she was busy working on designing some of her own quilting patterns.

As Lynda worked on and reviewed books by other authors, she saw a need for quilting designs on different topics—including cute designs for children. Do you think having a new grandson had anything to do with that? Yes, I'm sure it did.

This is a book of quilting patterns that can be used by new quilters or those who have been quilting for years. If you quilt by hand, home sewing machine, or longarm machine, these designs will help you prove that quilting does make the quilt!

Bonnie K. Browning
AQS Executive Show Director,
Quilt instructor and certified quilt judge,
Author of nine quilting books published by AQS

introduction

Definition of quilting:

A coverlet or blanket made of two layers of fabric with a layer of cotton, wool, feathers, or down in between, all stitched firmly together, usually in a decorative crisscross design.

Stitching through layers of fabric and a filling so as to create a design.

American Heritage Dictionary
www.dictionary.reference.com

Okay... So...

Where do I quilt? All over, around pieces, in sashing, in borders, anywhere you want!

What design or motif to quilt? Single elements, simple designs, combined elements, complex patterns —*what's your fancy?* Anything goes.

What style of quilting should I use? Traditional, modern, whimsical, *as long as you are happy with the finished project*. That is all that matters.

These are the questions that a lot of quilters ask after finishing a quilt top.

In answer, I have designed patterns that I think will solve some of the confusion of what to quilt where.

These patterns are only suggestions.

Whether you quilt by hand or use a shortarm, midarm, or longarm machine to quilt, these patterns are suitable for any quilting technique.

You can take them apart, combine elements from different patterns, omit elements and use only the part of the design *that appeals to you*. I give you a few ideas, then you use these designs in whatever way you want.

Select single flowers, leaves, or motifs from the designs for corners, sashing intersections or keystones in your quilt. Use the continuous vining designs for sashing or borders.

Enlarge or reduce the designs as needed to fit the different areas of your quilt.

When marking your quilt, use the method that is the most comfortable for your personal style—whether it is using water-soluble pens, graphite pencils, tracing paper, or quilting paper.

Use any color of thread that you like—solid or variegated, coordinating or contrasting—to make the quilting designs pop. The choice is yours. Make it pleasing to *your* eye.

These patterns and motifs could be used for other projects too. Use them for stencils, painted projects, stamping, scrapbooking—the possibilities are endless.

Quilting should be enjoyable, gratifying, and fun.

So don't sweat it...just **Quilt This!**

gardens & woods

Lotus

Lynda Smith

QUiLt ThiS!

Lotus Square

Deco Floral Vine

Lynda Smith

QUiLt ThiS!

Lynda Smith

QuiLt ThiS!

Leaves & Acorns

Lynda Smith

Quilt This!

Amber's Hibiscus

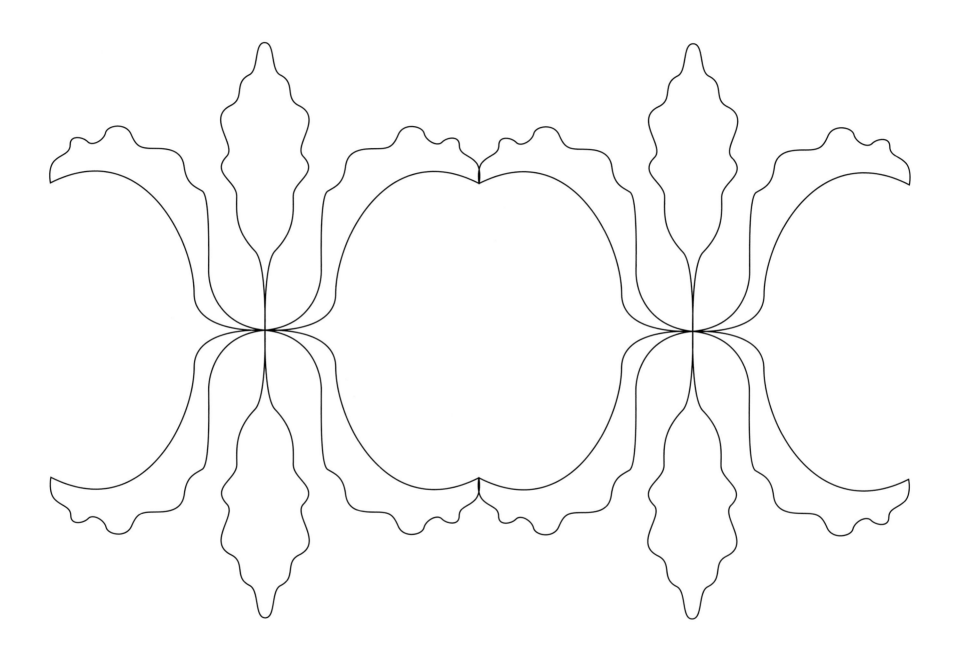

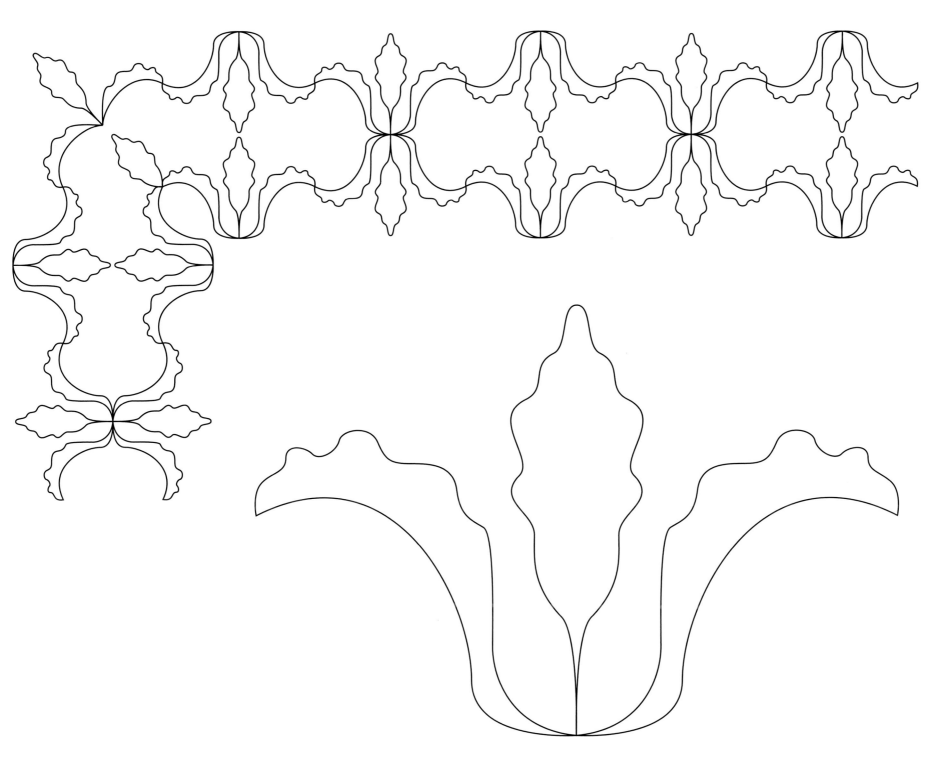

Lynda Smith

QuiLt ThiS!

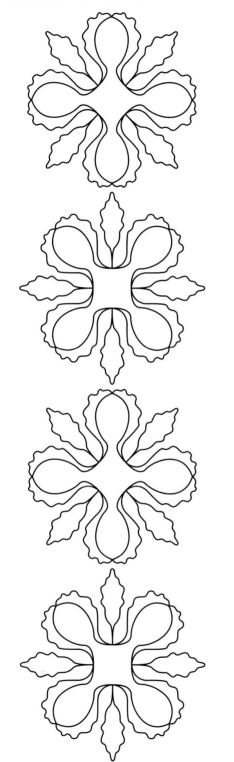

Bird's Nest Fern Medallion

Clover Border

Clover Square

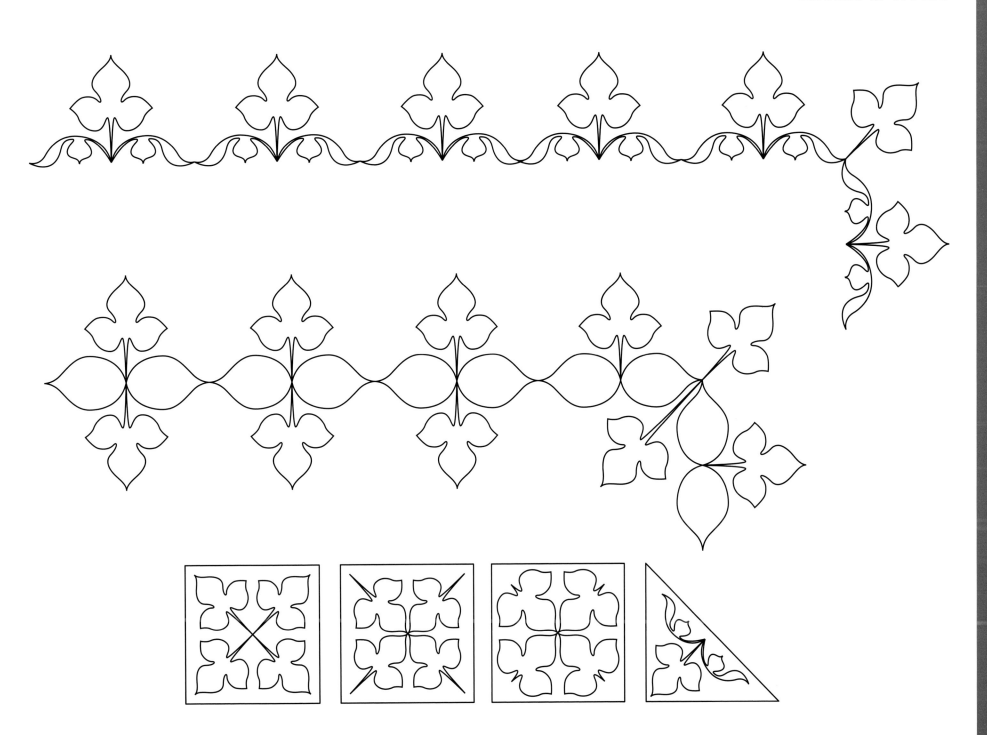

Lynda Smith

QuiLt ThiS!

Dogwood Trail

Lynda Smith

Lynda Smith

QUiLt ThiS!

Bleeding Heart

Lynda Smith

QUILT ThiS!

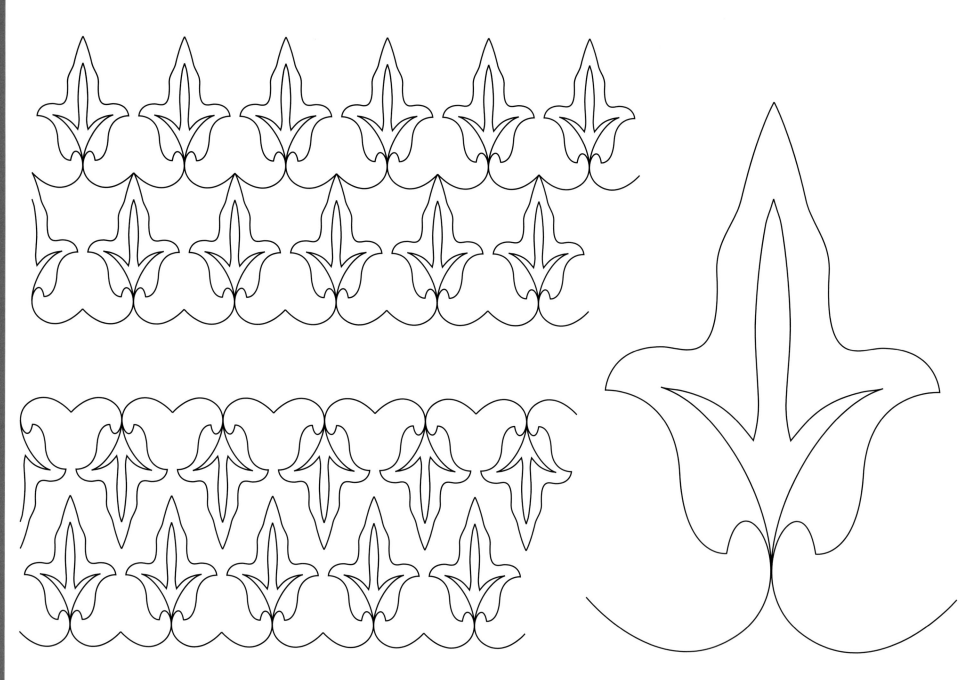

Ivy

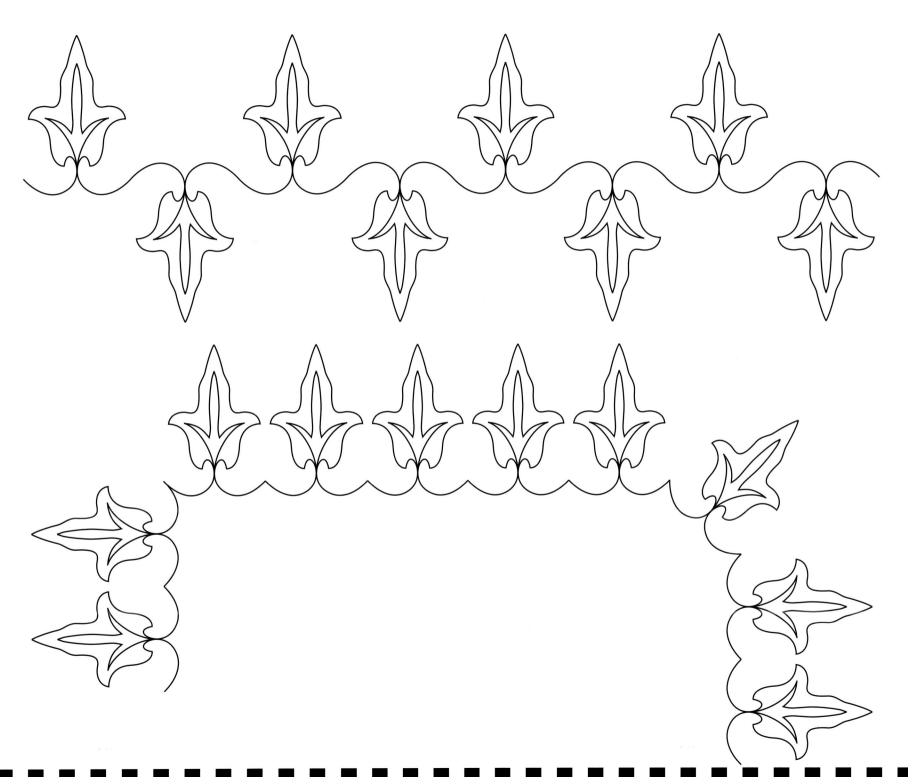

Ivy Square

Lynda Smith

QUiLt ThiS!

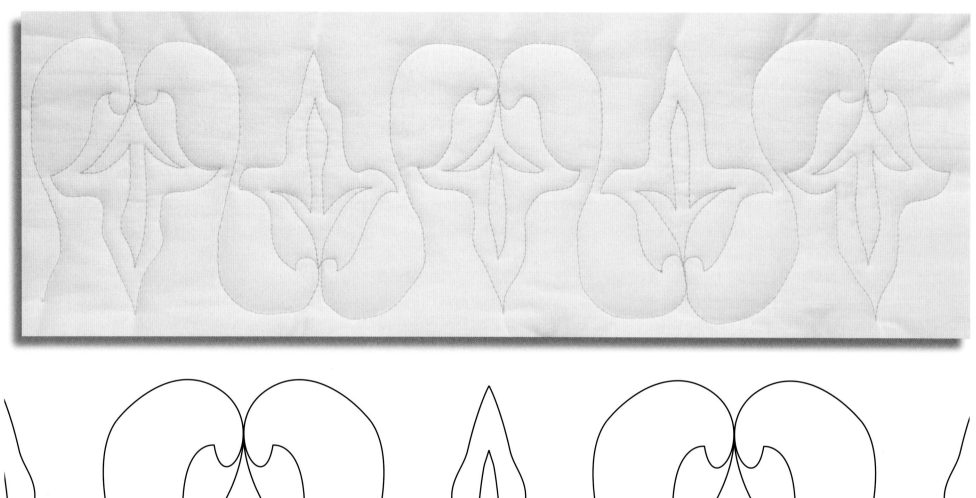

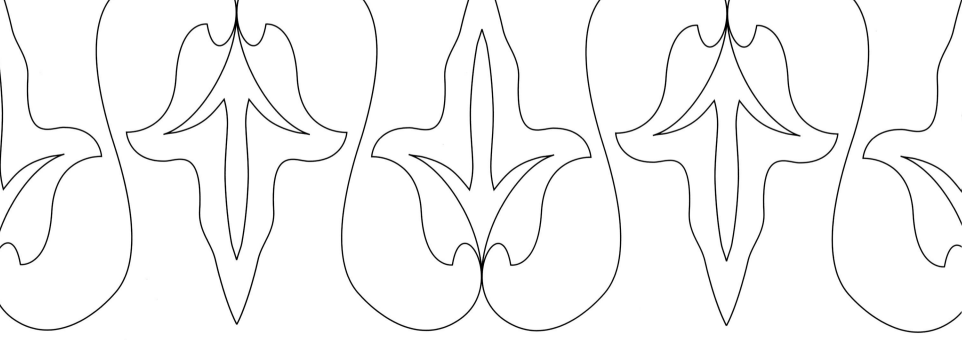

Trailing Ivy

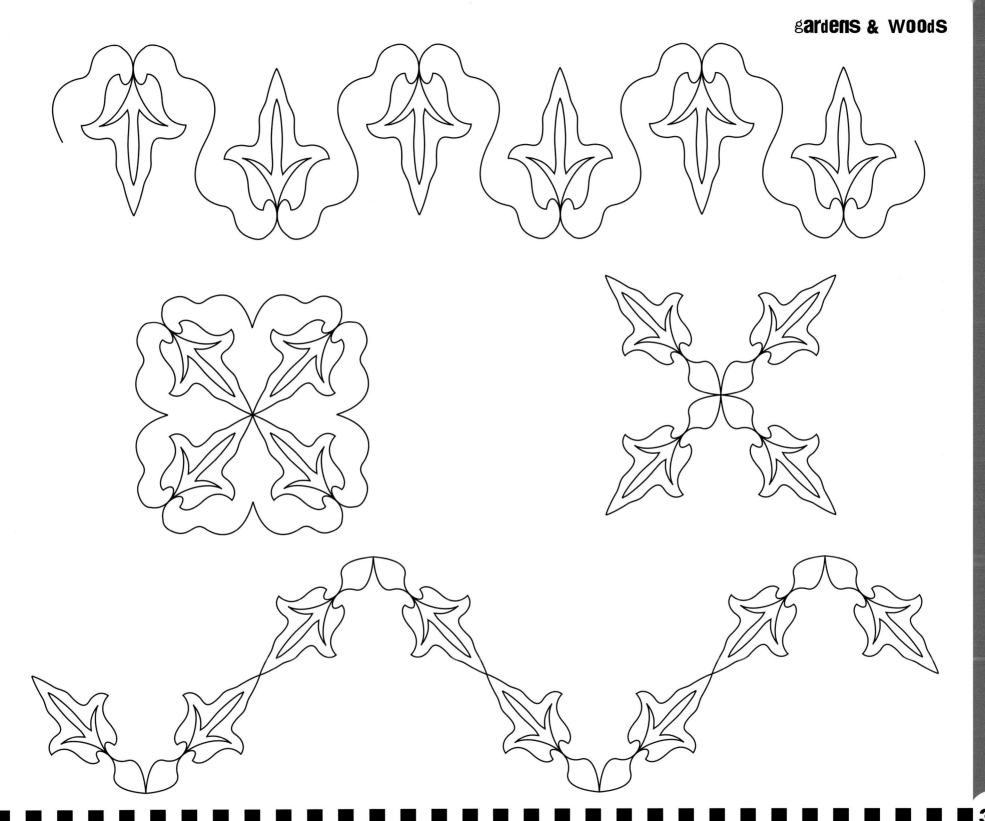

Crazy Ivy

Lynda Smith

QUilt This!

Tulip Patch

Tulip Patch Square

Lynda Smith

QuiLt ThiS!

Tulip Patch Explosion

Ivy Meander

QUILt ThIS!

Lynda smith

Trailing Ivy Meander

SWiRLS & CURLS

Elegant Leaves

QuiLt This!

Lynda Smith

QUiLt ThiS!

Quilt This!

Lynda Smith

Helen's Hints Square

Lynda Smith

QuiLt ThiS!

Arabesque

QUiLt ThiS!

Lynda Smith

Deco Shells

Lynda Smith

QuiLt ThiS!

Deco Shells Pair

MOtifS & Other StUff

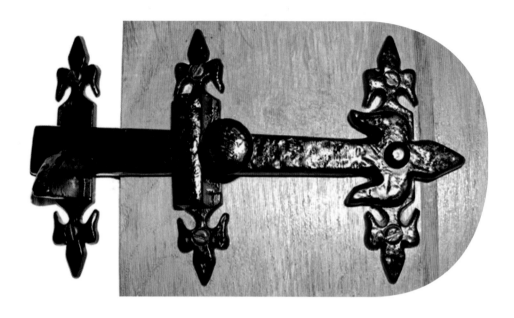

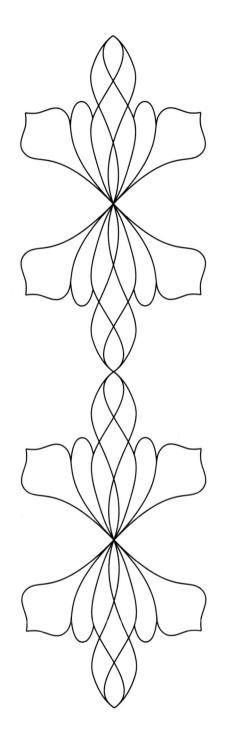

Frond Solo

Lynda Smith

QUiLt ThiS!

Eggs & Diamonds

Lynda Smith

QuiLt ThiS!

Chrystal's Crystal

Lynda Smith

QuiLt ThiS!

Water Drop

Lynda Smith

QuiLt ThiS!

Fleur de Wreath

Lynda Smith

QUiLt ThiS!

Lynda Smith

QUiLt ThiS!

Bull's Horn Circle

Temple Flower

Quilt This!

Lynda Smith

Temple Flower Square

Lynda Smith

QUiLt ThiS!

Modern Fern

Quilt This!

Lynda Smith

Lynda Smith

QuiLt ThiS!

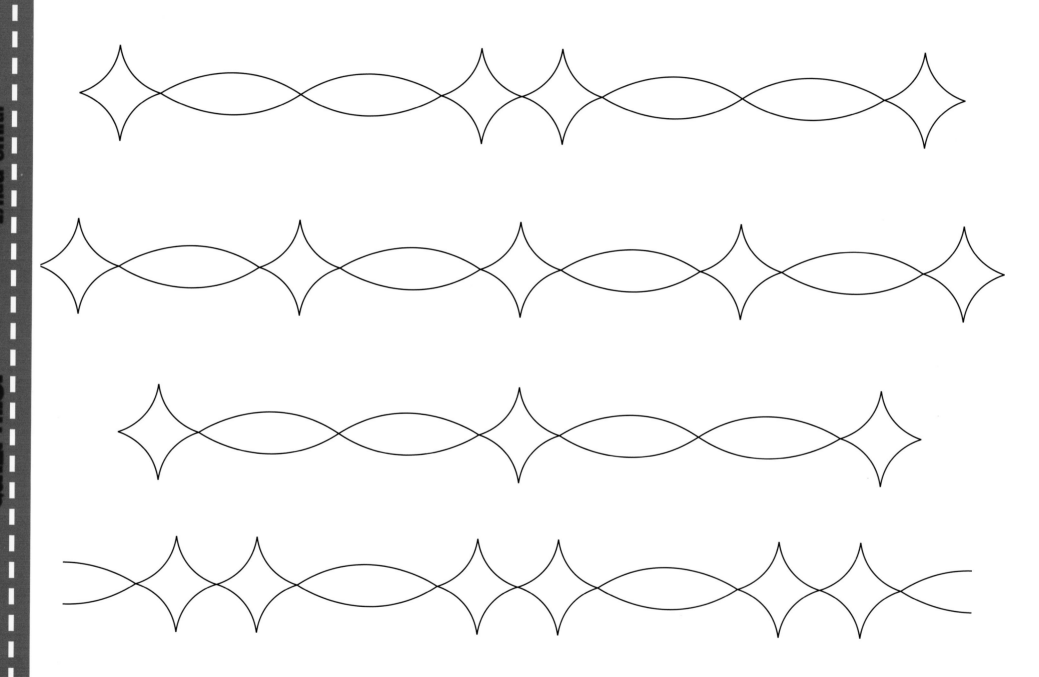

Points & Curves

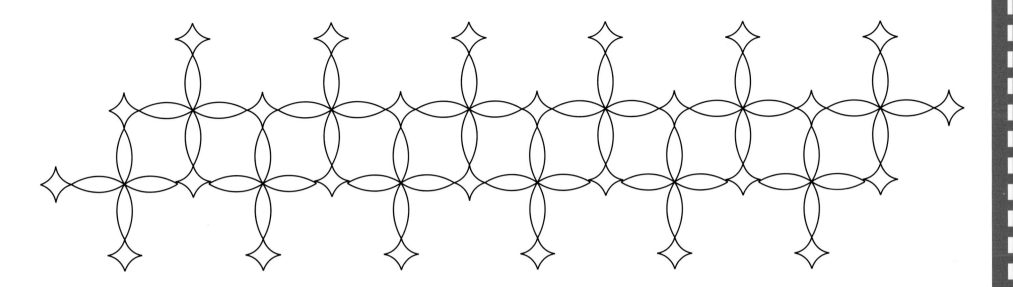

Lynda Smith

QUiLt ThiS!

Finial

QUiLt ThiS!

Lynda Smith

Firecracker

QUiLt ThiS!

Lynda Smith

Stars & Ice Explosion

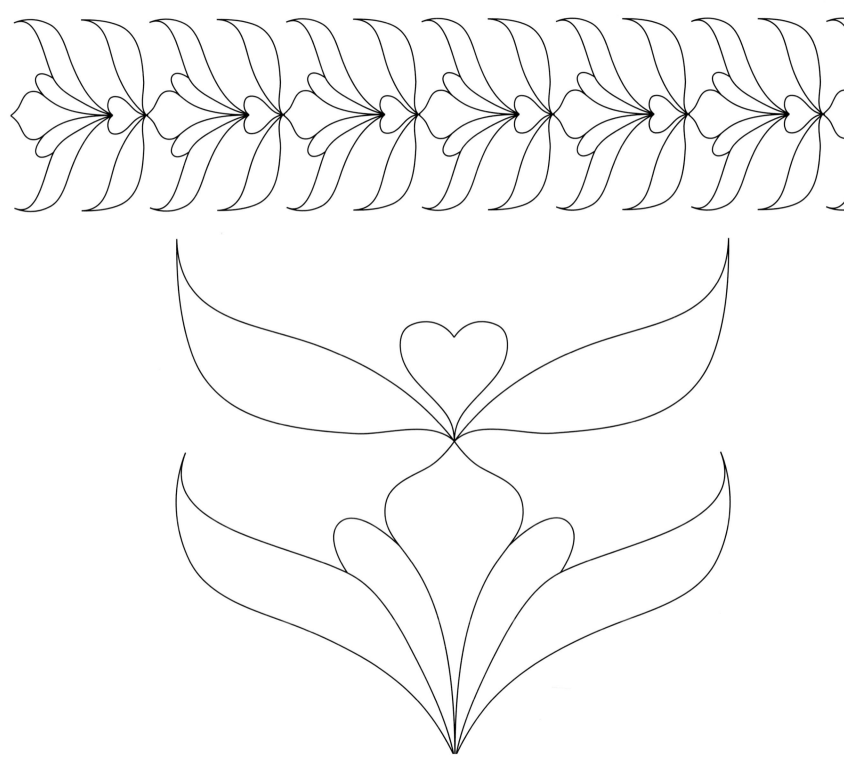

Children & Playtime

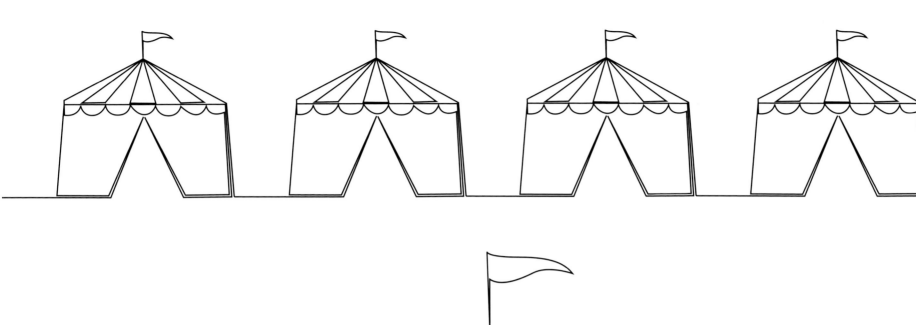

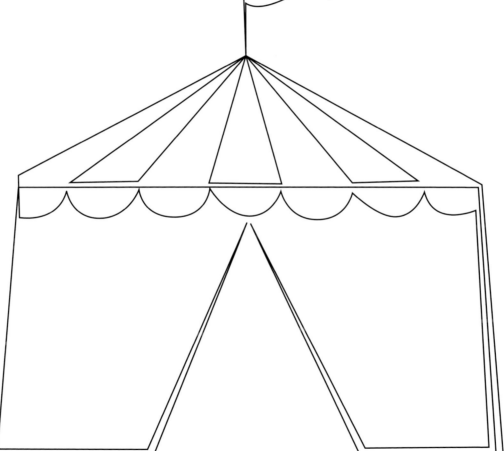

QUILT THIS!

Lynda Smith

Circus Tent

Lynda Smith

QUiLt ThiS!

Elephant Parade

Quilt This!

Lynda Smith

Quilt This!

Tyler's Seaworld

QUILt ThiS!

Circus Fun

QUiLt ThiS!

Don's Tools

about me!

Since I was born and raised in Paducah, Kentucky, home of the American Quilter's Society — Quilt City USA® — it must have been destiny for me to land my dream job of graphic designer for AQS.

During my eight years of working for AQS, I have designed over 50 books and worked 16 quilt shows in Paducah and Nashville. I have also learned a lot about quilting from some of the most notable quilters in the industry.

A quilter at heart, I was thrilled when my first-ever quilt, LOVELY PINK, was published in *Borders & Finishing Touches 2*, by Bonnie K. Browning, American Quilter's Society, 2006.

Married for 29 years, my husband, Donnie, and I have two wonderful children, Brian and Michael, and two fantabulous grandsons, Tyler and Aidan.

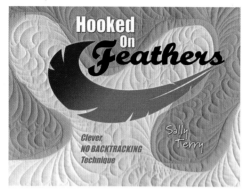
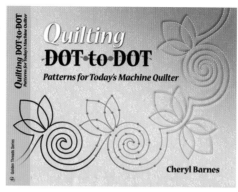
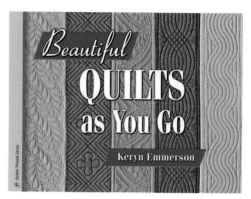
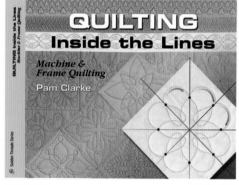

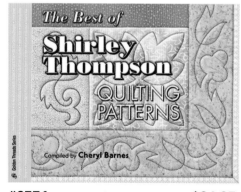

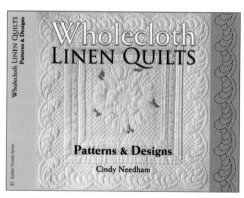